THREAD OF HUMANITY

"Unraveling the Tapestry of Life"
A Journey of Connection, Empathy, and Unity

Wasiu Fatosa

CONTENT

INTRODUCTION

In the vast tapestry of existence, there lies a thread that unites us all - the enigmatic thread of humanity. It weaves through the fabric of time, binding us together across continents, cultures, and generations. Welcome to a compelling and unique exploration of "The Thread of Humanity," an eBook that unravels the intricacies of our shared human experience. In this journey of self-discovery and connection, we embark on a voyage to understand the essence of what makes us human and the compelling force that shapes our collective way of life.

As we venture forth into this fascinating exploration, we find ourselves drawn to the whispers of ancient wisdom and the echoes of modern revelations. We traverse through the shadows of our past, unearthing forgotten tales and untold histories, and emerge into the vibrant tapestry of our present - a mosaic of triumphs and tribulations, joys and sorrows.

Within these pages, we shall encounter the extraordinary threads that weave together the essence of who we are - the threads of empathy that bind hearts, the threads of resilience that lift us beyond adversity, and the threads of compassion that mend the broken strands of our lives.

But as we delve into the depths of our shared humanity, we shall also explore the complexities that challenge our connections. We confront the threads of prejudice that mar our unity, the threads of indifference that fray our bonds, and the threads of fear that threaten to unravel the very fabric of our existence.

Yet, amidst the delicate balance of these threads, we discover a profound truth - that within every human heart beats the rhythm of hope, the melody of love, and the symphony of shared dreams. It is this universal harmony that binds us together, transcending the boundaries that divide us and leading us towards the uncharted horizons of tomorrow.

Through captivating stories, intriguing insights, and thought-provoking revelations, "The Thread of Humanity" will challenge our perceptions, ignite our curiosity, and inspire us to reflect on the tapestry of our own lives. As we unravel the threads that connect us to one another, we will find our souls entwined with the millions of souls that have journeyed before us and those that will journey after us.

Dear reader, prepare yourself to embark on a voyage like no other - a voyage that will uncover the mysteries of our shared humanity, kindle the flames of empathy, and ignite the desire to cherish every delicate thread that makes us human. For within the very fabric of "The Thread of Humanity" lies the power to reshape our world and forge connections that will stand the test of time.

So, let us journey together, hand in hand, as we unveil the extraordinary story of "The Thread of Humanity." In this unfolding narrative, we will not only discover the essence of what it means to be human but also find a profound sense of unity that weaves us into the grand tapestry of life.

CHAPTER ONE

The Essence of Human Connection

In the bustling heart of a vibrant city, among the sea of faces that rush by, there lies an invisible thread that binds us all - the essence of human connection. It is the intangible force that draws us together, transcending barriers of language, culture, and distance. In this chapter, we unravel the profound significance of human connection and explore how it shapes our lives and defines our humanity.

Section 1: Threads that Bind
The tapestry of human connection begins with the simplest of threads - a smile, a nod, a shared laugh. In these seemingly ordinary moments, we find the roots of our interconnectedness. Through heartwarming anecdotes and personal reflections, we discover how these brief encounters have the power to brighten someone's day and leave an indelible mark on our own.

Section 2: Bridges of Empathy
Empathy, the golden thread of human connection, allows us to step into another's shoes and see the

world through their eyes. In this section, we delve into the profound impact of empathetic understanding. Through real-life stories of compassion and selflessness, we come to realize that empathy is the gateway to forging deeper connections with others, fostering a sense of unity that knows no bounds.

Section 3: The Digital Tapestry
In today's hyper-connected world, the threads of human connection have extended beyond physical boundaries. The advent of technology has woven a digital tapestry that enables us to reach across oceans and connect with individuals from all walks of life. But with this newfound connectivity comes both opportunities and challenges. We explore the implications of living in an interconnected era, where virtual encounters shape our perceptions of others and ourselves.

Section 4: The Power of Shared Experiences
Throughout history, shared experiences have been the loom upon which human connections are woven. From celebrations to shared grief, these moments of togetherness define the fabric of our communities. In this section, we uncover how shared experiences create bonds that transcend

time, reminding us of the enduring strength of human connection.

Section 5: Embracing Diversity
The threads of human connection come in a myriad of colors, reflecting the diversity of our world. In this segment, we celebrate the beauty of cultural exchange and the richness that different perspectives bring to our lives. Through thought-provoking stories, we embrace the transformative power of embracing diversity and find strength in our shared humanity.

Section 6: The Impact of Small Acts
It is often the seemingly insignificant acts of kindness that create the strongest bonds. From the stranger who offers a helping hand to the friend who lends a listening ear, these small gestures create a web of compassion that weaves through our lives. In this section, we explore how these simple acts have the power to change lives and create a ripple effect of positivity in our interconnected world.

Section 7: The Threads of Trust
At the core of human connection lies trust - the delicate thread that weaves relationships together. We delve into the complexities of trust, examining

how it is built, shattered, and rebuilt in our personal and societal interactions. Through honest reflections and inspiring tales of resilience, we understand the significance of trust in nurturing our connections with others.

Section 8: The Threads that Heal
In moments of sorrow and pain, it is the threads of human connection that offer solace and support. In this section, we explore how acts of empathy and compassion can heal wounds, mend broken hearts, and provide strength during life's darkest moments. Through powerful stories of resilience and unity, we witness the profound impact of human connection in times of adversity.

Conclusion
As we conclude this chapter, we marvel at the intricacies and beauty of the essence of human connection. From the simple smiles that brighten our day to the deep bonds that sustain us through life's trials, we recognize that our lives are woven together in a magnificent tapestry of shared experiences and emotions.
In the threads that bind us, we find solace, strength, and the realization that we are never truly alone. As we continue our journey through this eBook, may the essence of human connection inspire you to

cherish and nurture the connections that enrich your life and seek out new threads that foster understanding, empathy, and unity with your fellow human beings. For in embracing our interconnectedness, we discover the true essence of what it means to be human.

CHAPTER TWO

Threads of Empathy and Understanding

In the rich tapestry of human connections, there exists a thread that serves as the bedrock of our shared humanity - the threads of empathy and understanding. As we delve into this chapter, we find ourselves stepping into the shoes of others, embracing their joys and sorrows, and connecting with the core of their experiences. Here, we explore the profound impact of empathy and understanding in shaping our relationships, fostering compassion, and breaking down barriers that often divide us.

Section 1: The Power of Walking in Another's Shoes
Empathy is the thread that weaves the fabric of human connection with the golden threads of understanding. In this section, we embark on a journey to uncover the roots of empathy and its transformative potential. Through real-life accounts of empathy's profound impact, we come to understand that the simple act of acknowledging and validating someone else's emotions can create bridges of understanding that transcend the boundaries of our differences.

Section 2: Compassion in Action
Empathy is the seed from which compassion blooms. In this part of the chapter, we explore how empathy transforms into action, propelling us to reach out and make a difference in the lives of others. We encounter heartwarming stories of individuals and communities coming together to support those in need, revealing the ripple effect of compassion that spreads far beyond the initial act of kindness.

Section 3: Bridging Divides
Empathy is the thread that can mend the divides that fragment our world. In this section, we confront the challenges of understanding perspectives different from our own. Through introspective reflections and examples of transformative dialogues, we learn that empathy is the key to bridging cultural, social, and ideological gaps, fostering an environment of mutual respect and appreciation.

Section 4: The Empathetic Leader
In leadership, empathy serves as a guiding thread, nurturing an environment of trust and collaboration. We explore the role of empathy in effective leadership, delving into the stories of leaders who

have leveraged empathy to create positive change. From corporate boardrooms to grassroots movements, we witness the remarkable power of empathetic leaders in shaping a better world.

Section 5: Empathy in Healthcare
In the realm of healthcare, empathy is the thread that ties together patients and caregivers, humanizing the healing process. In this section, we explore the vital role of empathy in medical practice, where the ability to understand and connect with patients can have a profound impact on their well-being. We uncover the experiences of both patients and healthcare providers to appreciate the profound effects of empathy in the healing journey.

Section 6: The Empathy Deficit
Despite its potential for positive change, empathy faces challenges in a world that sometimes seems to be losing touch with its compassionate core. In this part of the chapter, we confront the empathy deficit that plagues our societies, leading to isolation and discord. Through poignant stories and reflections, we delve into the roots of this deficit and

explore strategies to rekindle the empathetic flame within us all.

Section 7: Empathy through Art and Storytelling
Art and storytelling serve as powerful mediums to nurture empathy and understanding. In this section, we examine the transformative nature of literature, music, and visual arts in evoking emotions and expanding our perspectives. Through the works of artists who dared to challenge societal norms and inspire empathy, we discover how creative expressions can mend the tapestry of humanity.

Conclusion:
In the conclusion of this chapter, we marvel at the transformative power of empathy and understanding - the threads that bind us together as a compassionate human family. We reflect on the beauty of embracing diverse experiences and perspectives, finding solace in our shared joys and sorrows.
As we continue our journey through the fabric of "Threads of Empathy and Understanding," may we carry this newfound understanding into our daily lives, seeking out opportunities to connect with one another on a deeper level. Let us celebrate the threads that foster compassion, empathy, and understanding, for it is through these threads that

we strengthen the very foundation of our shared humanity. As we step into the next chapter of our exploration, may the empathy and understanding we cultivate be the guiding light that illuminates our path forward.

CHAPTER THREE

Threads of Resilience and Hope

In the intricate tapestry of human existence, there exists a thread that shines with unwavering strength and radiance - the threads of resilience and hope. As we delve into this chapter, we bear witness to the stories of courage, determination, and unwavering optimism that have woven this thread through the fabric of our lives. Here, we explore the profound impact of resilience and hope in navigating the challenges of life, transforming adversity into opportunity, and igniting the flame of hope that guides us through even the darkest of times.

Section 1: Triumph Over Adversity
Resilience is the thread that empowers us to rise above adversity, transforming trials into triumphs. In this section, we encounter tales of individuals who have faced immense challenges - from personal tragedies to formidable obstacles. Through their stories of resilience and perseverance, we learn how the human spirit can triumph over even the most daunting of circumstances, leaving an indelible mark on the tapestry of humanity.

Section 2: Finding Light in the Darkness
Hope is the golden thread that illuminates our path through the darkest moments of life. In this part of the chapter, we delve into the transformative power of hope, exploring how it sustains us during times of uncertainty and despair. Through the stories of those who have clung to hope in the face of adversity, we come to understand that hope is not a fleeting emotion but a guiding force that empowers us to move forward with courage.

Section 3: Building Resilience Through Connection
In the threads of resilience and hope, we find the strength that comes from connection and community. In this section, we explore how the support of others can bolster our resilience and nurture hope in times of crisis. Through the experiences of individuals who have found solace in the embrace of their communities, we witness the transformative nature of collective resilience.

Section 4: The Power of Mindset
Our mindset is the loom upon which resilience and hope are woven. In this part of the chapter, we delve into the psychology of resilience, exploring the factors that shape our ability to bounce back from adversity. Through scientific insights and

personal anecdotes, we discover the power of a positive outlook in nurturing resilience and fostering hope.

Section 5: Embracing Change with Hope
Change is an ever-present thread in the tapestry of life, and it is through hope that we embrace its winds of transformation. In this section, we explore how hope serves as an anchor in times of change, empowering us to adapt, grow, and find new opportunities amid uncertainty. From stories of reinvention to tales of transformation, we learn that hope is the compass that guides us through uncharted territories.

Section 6: The Resilience of Nature
Nature herself is a testament to resilience, as she endures the ebb and flow of seasons and cycles. In this part of the chapter, we draw inspiration from the natural world, exploring the threads of resilience that run through ecosystems and the interconnectedness of all living beings. We find solace in the wisdom of nature and the lessons she offers in resilience and hope.

Section 7: Nurturing Resilience and Hope in Others

As we reflect on the threads of resilience and hope in our own lives, we discover the profound impact of nurturing these qualities in others. In this section, we explore the role of caregivers, mentors, and communities in fostering resilience and instilling hope in those facing challenges. We witness the power of empathy and understanding in guiding others towards a path of strength and optimism.

Conclusion:
As we conclude this chapter, we are left with a deep appreciation for the threads of resilience and hope that strengthen the tapestry of humanity. We recognize that, in our collective journey through life, resilience empowers us to weather the storms, while hope lights our way towards a brighter tomorrow.
May the stories of resilience and hope woven into this chapter inspire us to face life's challenges with unwavering courage and optimism. As we continue our exploration through the fabric of humanity, may we carry the threads of resilience and hope within our hearts, empowering ourselves and others to persevere through adversity and embrace the promise of a better, more hopeful future.

CHAPTER FOUR

Threads of Cultural Diversity

In the intricate tapestry of humanity, there exists a vibrant and colorful thread - the threads of cultural diversity. This chapter celebrates the beautiful tapestry of cultures that enrich our world, weaving stories of traditions, customs, and histories that have shaped the unique identities of different communities. As we explore the richness of cultural diversity, we come to appreciate the threads that create the mosaic of humanity, fostering mutual understanding, appreciation, and a sense of unity in our global village.

Section 1: Embracing the Melting Pot
The tapestry of cultural diversity begins with the intermingling of different threads, creating a cultural melting pot. In this section, we celebrate the dynamic nature of culture and how diverse threads come together to shape new traditions and practices. We explore the beauty of cultural fusion, where the harmonious coexistence of customs from

different origins enriches our collective human experience.

Section 2: The Wisdom of Ancestral Threads
Each culture carries within it the wisdom of ancestral threads - the teachings, beliefs, and values passed down through generations. In this part of the chapter, we delve into the wealth of knowledge and heritage that resides within cultural traditions. Through captivating stories and historical anecdotes, we gain insight into the threads that have guided human societies for centuries.

Section 3: The Tapestry of Festivals and Celebrations
Festivals and celebrations are the vibrant threads that add splashes of color to the fabric of cultural diversity. In this section, we immerse ourselves in the joyous festivities of different cultures. From colorful carnivals to solemn religious observances, we explore how these celebrations foster a sense of identity and belonging, creating shared experiences that bind communities together.

Section 4: The Threads of Language and Communication
Language serves as a fundamental thread that defines cultural identity and facilitates

communication between individuals and communities. In this part of the chapter, we celebrate the diversity of languages spoken around the world, recognizing that each language carries within it unique expressions and nuances that reflect the essence of its culture. We explore the power of language in preserving traditions and in bridging cultural divides.

Section 5: Cultural Threads in Arts and Creativity
The arts are the creative threads that illuminate the tapestry of cultural diversity. In this section, we revel in the various art forms that reflect the essence of different cultures. From traditional dances that recount ancient stories to the mesmerizing melodies that evoke cultural pride, we discover how artistic expressions transcend borders, touching the hearts of people from diverse backgrounds.

Section 6: The Threads of Gastronomy
The culinary delights of different cultures weave together the threads of gastronomic diversity. In this part of the chapter, we embark on a culinary journey, savoring the unique flavors and aromas of dishes from around the world. We explore how food

acts as a cultural connector, bringing people together and igniting conversations that celebrate diversity.

Section 7: Cultural Threads in Architecture and Design

Architecture and design are the threads that shape the physical landscapes of cultures. In this section, we marvel at the diverse architectural styles that bear witness to the history, beliefs, and values of different societies. From towering temples to intricate palaces, we recognize that the art of design weaves tales of cultural identity and innovation.

Section 8: Celebrating Similarities and Embracing Differences

In our exploration of cultural diversity, we discover that amidst the varied threads, there are common elements that unite us all as humans. In this final section, we celebrate the similarities that bind us together, emphasizing the universal themes of love, family, and the pursuit of happiness. We also reflect on the importance of embracing differences, recognizing that it is in our diversity that we find the true beauty of humanity's fabric.

Conclusion:

As we conclude this chapter, we stand in awe of the kaleidoscope of cultural diversity that paints the tapestry of humanity. Each thread, woven by the hands of history and shaped by the hearts of generations, contributes to the symphony of life that weaves us all together. Let us celebrate the cultural diversity that enriches our lives, fostering understanding, tolerance, and appreciation for the myriad colors and textures that make up the beautiful mosaic of humanity. As we carry these insights forward, may we cherish the threads of cultural diversity, nurturing a world where all cultures are celebrated and all hearts find harmony in the global chorus of humanity.

CHAPTER FIVE

Threads of Shared Dreams and Aspirations

Within the grand tapestry of humanity, there exists a thread that transcends borders and unites hearts - the threads of shared dreams and aspirations. In this chapter, we embark on a journey through the aspirations that bind us together, transcending cultural, societal, and geographical boundaries. Here, we explore the power of collective dreams and the threads that weave our individual hopes into the fabric of a better world.

Section 1: The Universality of Dreams
Dreams are the universal language of the human spirit, transcending the barriers of language and culture. In this section, we reflect on the commonality of dreams and aspirations shared by people across the globe. From the pursuit of love and happiness to the desire for a better future, we discover the threads that unite us in our longing for a meaningful life.

Section 2: Nurturing Dreams in the Next Generation
The tapestry of shared dreams is sustained by the seeds of hope we plant in the next generation. In

this part of the chapter, we explore the pivotal role of parents, educators, and mentors in nurturing the aspirations of young minds. Through inspiring stories of individuals who have overcome obstacles to achieve their dreams, we understand the power of guidance and encouragement in shaping the dreams of tomorrow.

Section 3: Threads of Social Progress
Shared dreams act as catalysts for social progress and collective action. In this section, we delve into the historical narratives of movements that were ignited by shared aspirations for justice, equality, and human rights. From civil rights movements to environmental conservation efforts, we celebrate the threads of determination that have brought positive change to our world.

Section 4: The Threads of Innovation and Exploration
Humanity's progress has been driven by the threads of innovation and exploration. In this part of the chapter, we marvel at the dreams of visionaries who dared to imagine a world beyond the limits of the known. From space exploration to technological advancements, we witness the power of shared dreams that propel us towards new frontiers.

Section 5 Dreams that Transcend Generations
Some dreams stand the test of time, passing through the hands of generations like a precious thread. In this section, we pay homage to the enduring dreams and bournes that have shaped mortal history. From dreams of freedom to dreams of knowledge, we uncover the dateless vestments that connect us to our ancestors and the dreams they carried.

Section 6: The Dreamers Who Ignite Change
In the tapestry of shared dreams, there are individuals whose aspirations ignite transformation on a global scale. In this part of the chapter, we explore the stories of change-makers who have dared to dream and act for the greater good. Through their courage and tenacity, we learn that even a single thread of aspiration can weave a powerful narrative of hope for humanity.

Section 7: The Threads of Collaborative Endeavors
Shared dreams bring people together in collaborative endeavors, demonstrating the strength of unity. In this section, we celebrate the threads of collective action that unite individuals and communities in pursuit of common goals. From humanitarian efforts to global initiatives for a

sustainable future, we uncover the remarkable impact of collaboration in fulfilling shared dreams.

Section 8: Dreams That Inspire Resilience

In the face of challenges, shared dreams act as beacons of resilience. In this final part of the chapter, we discover how shared aspirations can provide solace and strength during difficult times. We witness the transformative power of hope and determination, igniting sparks of resilience that propel us forward on the path to realizing our shared dreams.

Conclusion:

As we conclude this chapter, we marvel at the intricate tapestry of shared dreams and aspirations that unite humanity as one. From the smallest aspirations to the grandest visions, each thread weaves a story of hope and possibility. Let us cherish the threads of shared dreams that connect us, for it is through these collective aspirations that we find the courage to embrace change, to forge ahead in unity, and to create a brighter, more harmonious world for all.

As we journey onward through the fabric of humanity, may the threads of shared dreams inspire us to listen to each other's yearnings, to support one another's aspirations, and to weave our individual hopes into the beautiful tapestry of a shared future. Together, let us envision a world where dreams are realized, and the threads of shared aspirations bring us closer to a world of peace, understanding, and boundless possibilities.

CHAPTER SIX

Threads of Love and Compassion

In the rich tapestry of human connections, the threads of love and compassion stand out as the most profound and transformative. This chapter explores the intricacies of these threads, as they weave through our lives, touching hearts, and creating bonds that transcend time and space. Love and compassion are the threads that define our humanity, nurturing our souls, and bringing warmth to the fabric of our shared existence.

Section 1: The Power of a Compassionate Heart
Compassion is the thread that binds us together in our shared humanity. In this section, we delve into the essence of compassion, understanding how it emerges from empathy and manifests as an act of genuine care for others. Through inspiring stories of compassion in action, we witness the remarkable impact of even the smallest acts of kindness on the lives of others.

Section 2: The Threads of Unconditional Love
Love is the thread that weaves the fabric of our closest relationships. In this part of the chapter, we

explore the many dimensions of love - from the love of family and friends to the love that transcends romantic boundaries. Through personal anecdotes and reflections, we uncover the depth of human capacity for love and its ability to heal and transform.

Section 3: Compassion for Self and Others
To extend compassion to others, we must first nurture self-compassion. In this section, we contemplate the importance of being gentle with ourselves and recognizing our shared vulnerabilities. By embracing self-compassion, we open our hearts to offer genuine empathy and understanding to those around us.

Section 4: The Threads of Forgiveness
Forgiveness is a thread that mends the tapestry of relationships and fosters healing. In this part of the chapter, we explore the power of forgiveness in freeing ourselves from the burdens of resentment and anger. Through stories of reconciliation and forgiveness, we learn that forgiveness is not a sign of weakness but a profound act of strength and love.

Section 5: The Compassion of Strangers

Compassion knows no boundaries, as it extends to those we may never meet. In this section, we witness the compassion of strangers who reach out to help others in times of crisis and need. From humanitarian efforts to random acts of kindness, we see how the threads of compassion connect us all in a web of shared humanity.

Section 6: Love and Compassion in Adversity

In the face of adversity, love and compassion become beacons of hope. In this part of the chapter, we explore how love and compassion manifest in times of crisis and challenge. From communities coming together in times of disaster to individuals supporting one another through difficult times, we see how love and compassion fortify our resilience.

Section 7: Threads of Empathy and Healing

Empathy is the foundation upon which love and compassion flourish. In this section, we delve into the interplay between empathy, love, and healing. Through the experiences of individuals who have found solace in the empathy and compassion of others, we witness the transformative power of these threads in times of vulnerability.

Section 8: Compassion in Action: Social Impact

Compassion is a force that drives positive social change. In this final part of the chapter, we explore how love and compassion motivate individuals and communities to take action for the betterment of society. From grassroots movements to global initiatives, we discover the collective power of compassion to address social injustices and create a more compassionate world.

Conclusion:

As we conclude this chapter, we are left with a profound appreciation for the threads of love and compassion that unite us all as human beings. Love and compassion are not mere emotions; they are the threads that hold the fabric of humanity together. May we carry the lessons of this chapter in our hearts, nurturing love and compassion in our own lives and spreading these transformative threads to others.

Let us recognize the profound impact of even the smallest acts of kindness, for they have the power to mend hearts, heal wounds, and inspire change. As we continue our exploration through the fabric of humanity, may the threads of love and compassion guide our actions, enrich our relationships, and create a world where empathy, understanding, and care weave us together as a global family.

CHAPTER SEVEN

Threads of Global Unity

In the grand tapestry of humanity, there exists a thread that stretches across continents, cultures, and borders - the threads of global unity. This chapter delves into the interconnectedness of our world, exploring the threads that bind us together as a global family. As we unravel the complexities of global unity, we discover the shared responsibilities, challenges, and aspirations that unite us in our collective journey towards a better future.

Section 1: Embracing Our Shared Home
The Earth is our shared home, and the thread of global unity reminds us of our interconnectedness with the planet and all its inhabitants. In this section, we explore the threads of environmental stewardship and the collective responsibility to protect and preserve our planet for future generations. We witness the transformative impact of global initiatives aimed at addressing climate change and creating a sustainable world.

Section 2: The Web of Interconnected Economies

Economic threads weave together the fortunes of nations, creating a web of interconnected economies. In this part of the chapter, we delve into the global trade networks and financial systems that shape the flow of goods, services, and capital across borders. We contemplate the challenges and opportunities of economic interdependence and the importance of fostering equitable global economic growth.

Section 3: Threads of Collaboration in Science and Innovation

The pursuit of knowledge and innovation knows no borders, as threads of collaboration in science and technology connect researchers and innovators worldwide. In this section, we explore the power of international cooperation in advancing scientific discoveries and technological breakthroughs. From collaborative space exploration to multinational research projects, we witness the potential of global unity in driving human progress.

Section 4: The Threads of Cross-Cultural Understanding

Cultural exchange is the thread that fosters cross-cultural understanding and appreciation. In this part of the chapter, we celebrate the diversity of cultures and the opportunities for intercultural dialogue and exchange. We explore the role of art, literature, and education in promoting cross-cultural understanding, cultivating empathy, and breaking down barriers that hinder global unity.

Section 5: Global Challenges, Shared Solutions
Global challenges require collective solutions. In this section, we confront the threads of poverty, inequality, and conflict that persist in different corners of the world. Through stories of humanitarian efforts and international collaborations, we witness the power of global unity in addressing these pressing issues and building a more just and equitable world.

Section 6: The Threads of Diplomacy and Cooperation
Diplomacy serves as the thread that weaves the fabric of international relations. In this part of the chapter, we explore the importance of diplomacy in resolving conflicts, fostering dialogue, and promoting peace. We witness the impact of multilateral institutions and collaborative efforts in finding common ground and working towards shared goals.

Section 7: Threads of Global Philanthropy and Humanitarianism
Humanitarian threads weave stories of compassion and generosity that traverse the globe. In this section, we celebrate the philanthropic endeavors and humanitarian initiatives that address global crises and uplift marginalized communities. From disaster relief efforts to long-term development projects, we uncover the immense impact of global solidarity and unity in humanitarian endeavors.

Section 8: Threads of Unity in Times of Crisis
In times of crisis, the threads of global unity shine brightest. In this final part of the chapter, we reflect on how the world comes together to face common challenges, such as pandemics, natural disasters, and humanitarian emergencies. We discover the resilience of humanity and the power of collective action in times of adversity.

Conclusion:
As we conclude this chapter, we are inspired by the threads of global unity that bind us together as a global family. The challenges we face are shared, and the solutions lie in our collective efforts. Let us embrace our interconnectedness, recognizing that the well-being of one part of the world affects us all.

As we continue our exploration through the fabric of humanity, may the threads of global unity guide us towards a world of cooperation, understanding, and compassion. Let us celebrate the threads that weave us together as one human family, for it is through global unity that we can create a world where peace, justice, and prosperity extend to every corner of the tapestry of humanity.

CHAPTER EIGHT

Threads of Legacy and Continuity

In the vast and intricate tapestry of human existence, there are threads that transcend time, leaving a lasting legacy for generations to come - the threads of legacy and continuity. In this chapter, we delve into the essence of these enduring threads, exploring how the actions and choices of individuals and societies shape the fabric of history and inspire a sense of continuity in the ever-evolving story of humanity.

Section 1: The Imprint of Ancestral Threads
The threads of legacy begin with the imprints left by our ancestors. In this section, we explore how the choices and achievements of previous generations ripple through time, influencing the paths we tread today. Through stories of historical figures and cultural pioneers, we witness how their legacies have shaped the values, traditions, and aspirations of contemporary societies.

Section 2: The Threads of Cultural Heritage
Cultural heritage is a thread that weaves together the tapestry of our identities. In this part of the

chapter, we celebrate the richness of cultural legacies, from ancient civilizations to indigenous traditions. We reflect on the importance of preserving cultural heritage, not only as a source of pride but as a bridge between generations, fostering continuity and understanding.

Section 3: Threads of Family and Generational Bonds

Family is a thread that ties together the chapters of our lives. In this section, we explore the significance of family ties and the ways in which intergenerational connections pass down values, stories, and wisdom. We discover the power of familial love and support in nurturing the threads of legacy within the fabric of our personal histories.

Section 4: The Threads of Education and Knowledge

Education is a thread that empowers individuals and societies to forge a path towards a better future. In this part of the chapter, we delve into the transformative role of education in passing down knowledge and shaping the dreams and aspirations of the next generation. We witness the impact of visionary educators and institutions in shaping the fabric of progress.

Section 5: The Threads of Artistic Expression
Art is a thread that weaves beauty and creativity into the tapestry of human history. In this section, we celebrate the artistic legacies that transcend time, from classical masterpieces to contemporary expressions. We explore how art serves as a mirror of society, reflecting the dreams, emotions, and values of the human experience.

Section 6: Threads of Technological Advancement
Technological advancements are threads that propel human civilization forward. In this part of the chapter, we explore the impact of innovation and technological breakthroughs on the fabric of progress. From the Industrial Revolution to the digital age, we witness how these threads have reshaped societies and ushered in new eras of continuity.

Section 7: The Threads of Social Change and Advocacy
The threads of legacy often emerge from the pursuit of social change and advocacy. In this section, we reflect on the lives of activists and visionaries who have championed causes for equality, justice, and human rights. We discover how their efforts have woven lasting legacies that inspire present and future generations to continue

the journey towards a more just and compassionate world.

Section 8: Threads of Continuity in the Face of Change
In times of change and uncertainty, threads of continuity provide a sense of stability and belonging. In this final part of the chapter, we explore the threads of continuity in the midst of shifting landscapes, from the preservation of natural ecosystems to the resilience of cultures and communities. We learn how embracing continuity helps us navigate the ever-changing currents of life.

Conclusion:
As we conclude this chapter, we recognize the significance of the threads of legacy and continuity in shaping the tapestry of human history. Each individual, each community, and each generation weaves a unique thread, leaving an indelible mark on the fabric of time. Let us honor the legacies of our ancestors, preserve our cultural heritage, and pass down the flame of knowledge to future generations.
As we journey through the intricate fabric of humanity, may the threads of legacy and continuity inspire us to live with purpose, to leave a positive imprint on the world, and to cherish the

interconnectedness that binds us together as a global family. Let us embrace our role as weavers of the future, recognizing that the threads we sow today will continue to ripple through time, shaping the destiny of humanity's grand tapestry.

CHAPTER NINE

Conclusion

As we reach the final stitches of this journey through the enchanting tapestry of humanity, we stand in awe of the myriad threads that bind us together as one global family. The chapters we've explored have revealed the intricate interplay of life's threads - from the cosmic origins to the tender threads of love and compassion that nurture our souls.

In the essence of human connection, we found that we are woven into a fabric of shared experiences, dreams, and aspirations. The Dance of Molecules taught us that life's intricate beauty emerges from the tiniest interactions, while the Threads of Resilience and Hope unveiled the strength of the human spirit in the face of adversity. We discovered that the colorful Threads of Cultural Diversity bring vibrancy to the tapestry of life, and Threads of Global Unity reminded us of our collective responsibility to create a world of peace and understanding.

The legacy of humanity stretches through the fabric of time, leaving an enduring imprint that touches every generation. Threads of legacy and continuity inspire us to preserve our cultural heritage, embrace change with resilience, and pave the way for a brighter tomorrow.

As we conclude our exploration, let us cherish the unbreakable bonds that unite us as human beings. Together, we weave a masterpiece of compassion, understanding, and unity. Each thread, no matter how small, is essential to the harmony of the whole. Just as the Weaver's Loom brought forth the grand design of existence, we too are weavers of our destiny, intricately connected, and responsible for each stitch.

As we move forward, let the Threads of Love and Compassion guide our actions, embracing the diversity of the world and fostering empathy for all living beings. Let us forge Threads of Global Unity that transcend borders, bridging differences and celebrating our shared humanity.

May this journey through the tapestry of humanity inspire us to tread lightly upon the Earth, nurturing Threads of Environmental Stewardship for the generations to come. Let the Threads of Legacy and Continuity inspire us to leave behind a world that is better than we found it.

In every thread, we find the potential to create a world where love triumphs over hatred, where understanding overcomes ignorance, and where compassion envelops all beings. The grand tapestry of humanity is a work in progress, an ever-evolving masterpiece guided by the hearts and hands of each and every one of us.

As we bid farewell to this exploration, may the Threads of Life's Tapestry continue to weave stories of wonder, compassion, and hope. Let us carry this knowledge with us, fostering unity and empathy in all our interactions, and creating a brighter, more harmonious world for the grand tapestry of humanity.

www.ingramcontent.com/pod-product-compliance
Lightning Source LLC
Chambersburg PA
CBHW071010260726
48661CB00007B/2877